I0485406

How Product Managers Can Learn To Understand Their Customers

Techniques For Product Managers To Better Understand What Their Customers Really Want

"Practical, proven examples of how to get the customer insights that are necessary in order to have a successful product"

Dr. Jim Anderson

Published by:
Blue Elephant Consulting
Tampa, Florida

Copyright © 2015 by Dr. Jim Anderson

All rights reserved. No part of this book may be reproduced of transmitted in any form or by any means, electronic or mechanical, including photocopying, recording or by any information storage and retrieval system without written permission of the publisher, except for inclusion of brief quotations in a review.

Printed in the United States of America

Library of Congress Control Number: 2015955764

ISBN-13: 978-1518768248
ISBN-10: 1518768245

Warning – Disclaimer

The purpose of this book is to educate and entertain. This book does not promise or guarantee that anyone following the ideas, tips, suggestions, techniques or strategies will be successful. The author, publisher and distributor(s) shall have neither liability nor responsibility to anyone with respect to any loss or damage caused, or alleged to be caused, directly or indirectly by the information contained in this book.

Recent Books By The Author

Product Management

- Product Management Secrets: Techniques For Product Managers To Boost Product Sales And Increase Customer Satisfaction

- Customer Lessons For Product Managers: Techniques For Product Managers To Better Understand What Their Customers Really Want

Public Speaking

- Secrets To Organizing A Speech For Maximum Impact: How to put together a speech that will capture and hold your audience's attention

- How To Become A Better Speaker By Changing How You Speak: Change techniques that will transform a speech into a memorable event

CIO Skills

- What CIOs Need To Know About Working With Partners: Techniques For CIOs To Use In Order To Be Able To Successfully Work With Partners

- How CIOs Can Make Innovation Happen: Tips And Techniques For CIOs To Use In Order To Make Innovation Happen In Their IT Department

IT Manager Skills

- Secrets Of Managing Budgets: What IT Managers Need To Know In Order To Understand How Their Company Uses Money

- Growing Your CIO Career: How CIOs Can Work With The Entire Company In Order To Be Successful

Negotiating

- All Good Things Come To An End: How To Close A Negotiation - How To Develop The Skill Of Closing In Order To Get The Best Possible Outcome From A Negotiation

- Learn How To Package Trades In Your Next Negotiation

Miscellaneous

- The Internet-Enabled Successful School District Superintendent: How To Use The Internet To Boost Parental Involvement In Your Schools

- Power Distribution Unit (PDU) Secrets: What Everyone Who Works In A Data Center Needs To Know!

Note: See a complete list of books by Dr. Jim Anderson at the back of this book.

Acknowledgements

Any book like this one is the result of years of real-world work experience. In my over 25 years of working for 7 different firms, I have met countless fantastic people and I've been mentored by some truly exceptional ones. Although I've probably forgotten some of the people who made me the person that I am today, here is my attempt to finally give them the recognition that they so truly deserve:

- Thomas P. Anderson
- Art Puett
- Bobbi Marshall
- Bob Boggs

Dr. Jim Anderson

This book is dedicated to my wife Lori. None of this would have been possible without her love and support.

Thanks for the best 21 years of my life (so far)...!

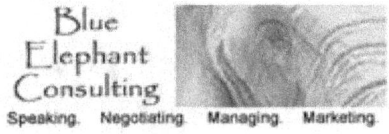

Table Of Contents

Do You Really Understand Your Customer?

If you want to be successful as a product manager than you are going to have to be able to create products that solve problems for your customers. In order to do this, you are going to first have to understand your customers – what are their wants and needs?

In order to be able to answer questions like this, you may find out that you are going to have to fire some of your customers – they are just too expensive for you to try to keep happy. Ultimately you want to change the relationship that you have with your customers and move towards being seen as more of a partner than a vendor.

In some cases, one of your customers may start to use your product too much. In these cases you'll need to be able to find a way to tell them to stop using it. You'll be able to do this if you've found a way to have a real relationship with your customer. However, along with this comes the risk of perhaps finding out too much about a given customer.

Once you have a customer, you may not have them forever. Customer loyalty is a fickle thing that product managers need to understand. One way to increase loyalty is to customize your product and engage in some niche marketing.

All customers are not created the same and so product managers need to take the time to understand their differences. This means learning to love the crazy ones or realizing that you may be selling primarily to grandparents. Take the time to study product managers who know how to do this right and in the end, make sure that you don't end up surprising your customers – nobody likes that!

For more information on what it takes to be a great product manager, check out my blog, The Accidental Product Manager, at:

www.TheAccidentalPM.com

Good luck!

-    Dr. Jim Anderson

About The Author

I must confess that I never set out to be a product manager. When I went to school, I studied Computer Science and thought that I'd get a nice job programming and that would be that. Well, at least part of that plan worked out!

My first job was working for Boeing on their F/A-18 fighter jet program. I spent my days programming fighter jet software in assembly language and I loved it. The U.S. government decided to save some money and went looking for other countries to sell this plane to. This put me into an unfamiliar role: I started to meet with foreign military officials in order to explain what my product did.

Time moved on and so did I. I found myself working for Siemens, the big German telecommunications company. They were making phone switches and selling them to the seven U.S. phone companies. The problem was that the switches were too complicated. Customers couldn't tell the difference between one complicated phone switch from another complicated phone switch.

The Siemens sales folks were in a bind. They didn't know enough about how the switches worked to tell their customers why they should buy them. Siemens reached out into their engineering unit looking for anyone who could help the sales teams out. I put my hand up and overnight I became a product manager.

Since then I've spent over 20 years working as a product manager for both big companies and startups. This has given me an opportunity to do everything that a product manager does many, many times. I know what works as well as what doesn't work.

I now live in Tampa Florida where I spend my time managing my consulting business, Blue Elephant Consulting, teaching college courses at the Florida Polytechnic University, and traveling to work with companies like yours to share the knowledge that I have about how product managers can make their product be a success.

I'm always available to answer questions and I can be reached at:

Dr. Jim Anderson
Blue Elephant Consulting
Email: jim@BlueElephantConsulting.com
Facebook: http://goo.gl/1TVoK
Web: **www.BlueElephantConsulting.com**

"Unforgettable communication skills that will set your ideas free..."

Create Products Your Customers Want At A Price That They Are Willing To Pay!

Dr. Jim Anderson is available to provide training and coaching on the two topics that are the most important to product managers everywhere: how do I create the products that my customers want and what should I price them at?

Dr. Anderson believes that in order to both learn and remember what he says, product managers need to laugh. Each one of his speeches is full of fun and humor so that what he says "sticks" with everyone.

Dr. Anderson's Product Management Training Includes:

1. How can you segment your market?
2. What problems are your customers having right now?
3. Which of your customer's problems does your product solve?
4. How much of this problem does your product solve?
5. How much will it cost your customer if they don't fix this problem?

Dr. Jim Anderson presents over 100 speeches per year. To invite Dr. Anderson to speak at your event, contact him at:

Phone: 813-418-6970 or
Email: jim@BlueElephantConsulting.com

Blue Elephant Consulting
Speaking. Negotiating. Managing. Marketing.

12

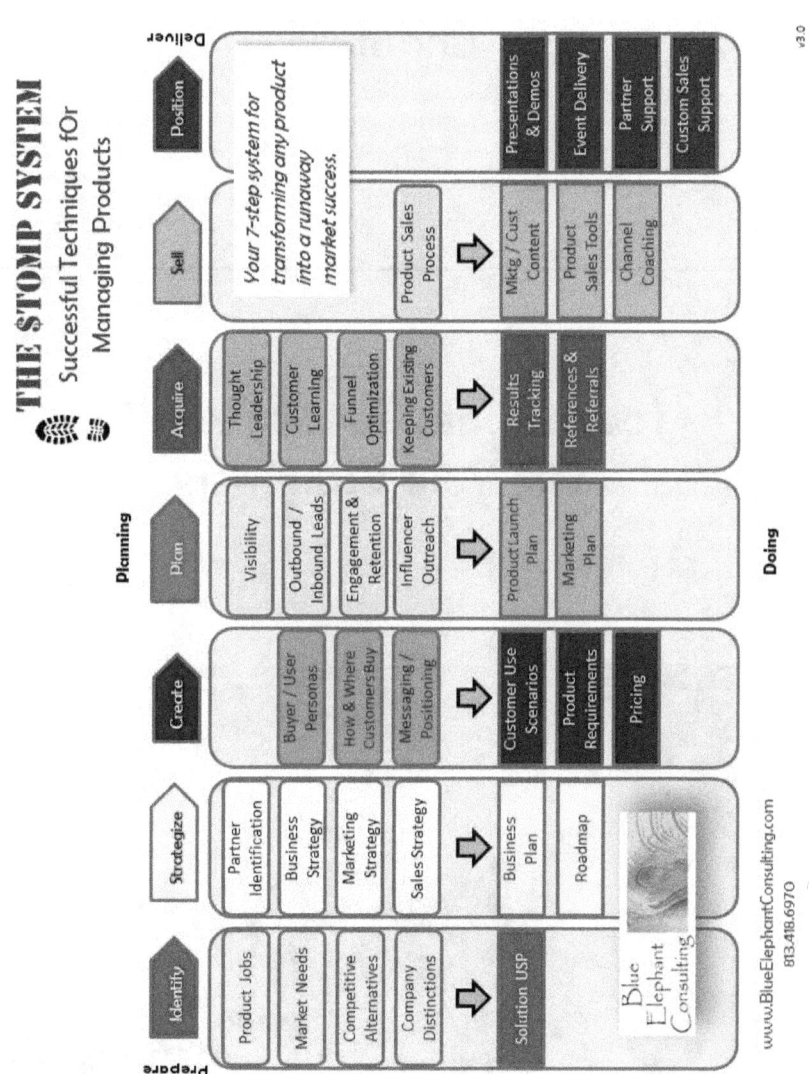

The **$TOMP** product management system has been created by **Blue Elephant Consulting** to help product managers know what to do and when to do it in order for a product to be successful.

13

Chapter 1

Tough Times Call For You To Fire Your Customers

Chapter 1: Tough Times Call For You To Fire Your Customers

Well, not all of them of course, but at least the ones that you really don't want to have. As product mangers we all like to brag both internally and externally about how many customers are using our products. However, the **dirty little secret** that we don't share is that all customers are not created equal. In these tough economic times we should finally get around to firing the bad ones...

What Makes A Customer A Bad Customer

Here's a novel idea: how about if you used your profitable customers to drive **more profit** to your company's bottom line? Who could argue with that? Well, there's a flip side to that coin: get rid of the customers who cost too much to serve.

Dr. Larry Selden of Columbia University has written the book on good customers and bad customers (Angel Customers and Demon Customers: Discover Which is Which and Turbo-Charge Your Stock). What his research has found is that the bottom 20% of customers can **drain your product's profits by 80%** while the top 20% can generate 150% of your product's profit.

Do I have you attention now? It sure looks like this would be a good time to spend some time **categorizing your customers**. You need to change the way that you do business as a product manager and stop being product-centric and become customer-centric (yeah, yeah — I know that you say that you already are, but you really aren't). The reality is that you can't serve every customer at the same level and you're spending too much time on the bad customers.

How To Find Your Bad Customers

If we are all in agreement that you probably have some customers that should be **shown to the door**, our next challenge is to find out just exactly which of your customers fit this profile. They like to hide amongst your good customers so they can be tricky to find.

The best way to smoke them out is to **categorize your customers**. There are lots of different ways to try to do this: demographics, geography, product purchases. However, if you do it this way then you're not going to find what you are looking for. Your bad customers will still be hiding from you.

Please note that finding your bad customers is not an easy task nor is it quick. You should plan on the process taking upwards of about **6 months** to complete. This is how long a well-done customer-profitability analysis takes if you segment your customer results into groups based on customer needs.

In order to do this kind of analysis, you are going to need **a lot of data**. This data will come from your cost data, individual sales records, and your customer demographics.

Once you've completed doing this analysis the right way you can then **rank your customers** from the least to the most profitable. This is a good start; however, you still need to take it one step further. What you need to do is to then segment your list of customers into groups based on what their needs are. This includes things like buying patterns, behaviors, and other types of information.

How To Fire Your Bad Customers

Once you've identified your unprofitable customers, it's time to deliver the bad news. However, wait a minute. What makes these customers bad customers is that they have **bad habits** when it comes to buying your products. You need to see if they are willing to change these habits and become good customers.

This means that you're going to have to sit down with them and **have a talk**. I suggest that you be frank with them and explain that it just doesn't make good business sense for you to keep doing business with them like you currently are.

There are lots of small changes that can be made that might change them into good customers. Changing the priority of things that you ship to them. Finding ways to reduce the number of calls that they make to your help desk. You need to include all of these in your discussion with them **before** you fire them for good.

What All Of This Means For You

The reason that product managers exist is to create and maintain profitable products. In a perfect world, you could focus all of your time and energy on deepening your relationship with your profitable customers. However, there's one small problem with this: **you have some bad customers**.

The challenge is in discovering which of your customers are the **bad ones**. If you take the time to roll up your sleeves and do some digging in the numbers that you already have, you can uncover which of your customers are the bad ones.

Once you've identified them, it's time to sit down and have a talk. If they are willing to change the way that they are doing business with you, then keep them. If not, then **it's time to let them go**. Breaking up can be tough to do, but in this case your product's bottom line will thank you for doing it.

Chapter 2

How To Move From Customers To Partners

Chapter 2: How To Move From Customers To Partners

As product managers, one of the things that we enjoy doing the most is sitting back and counting the number of customers that our product has. Although this is great fun to do, it's not really what we should be doing with our time. Customers are great to have, but it turns out that what we should really be doing is looking for ways to turn them into something much more valuable: **partners**.

What's Up With This Partner Thing?

If you have really been doing your job as a product manager, then you've already gone through your product's existing customers and "fired" those customers that were costing you more than you were making from them. What you are left with is (hopefully) a collection of traditionally good customers. Now you've got to get ready to make the **next step**.

What you've got to do is to find ways to **collaborate** with your customers. Sorry you self-centered product managers, this collaboration isn't about you, rather it's all about finding ways to help your product's customers become more profitable.

Exactly how best to do this is **going to depend** both on the business that your customer is in and what your product does for them. Collaboration could take the form of using your product to help your customer with their long-term planning, perhaps it can help address issues with their supply chain, etc.

Building A Bigger Box

All of us product managers suffer from a common fault. In our daily lives, the things that we work on can expand to **fill all of**

our available time. This includes tasks such as working with product development, creating new product collateral, picking new features, etc. What's missing from this is interaction with our customers.

The walls that make up our cube / office can easily start to define our world. If we want to start to collaborate with our customers, then we are going to have to **push those walls out** far enough so that our customers are now inside of our daily lives. It's only by doing this that we'll be able to find ways to get closer to our customers.

Can You Say Indispensable?

The difference between a customer and a partner is that you are simply another supplier to a customer whereas when you become a partner, then you have become **indispensable**. Your sales teams are working hard to make themselves indispensable to your customers, you need to be doing the same for your product.

Hopefully by now you've realized that you can't create this kind of deep relationship with all of your customers. You are going to have to sort the customers that you currently have and **select the few** that you'd like to move to being partners with.

Developing a partnership with your customers is difficult, maintaining it can be **even more challenging**. This will require more of your time; however, it's quite difficult to do this kind of relationship creation and so if you can pull it off, then you will have created a significant competitive advantage for your product.

What All Of This Means For You

Having customers for your product is fantastic. However, savvy product managers realize that just having customers is not enough. Instead, they know that they need to go to the extra effort **to turn some of those customers into partners**.

In order to create a partner for your product, you need to find ways to **collaborate with your customers**. This is all about them: how can you and your product help this customer to increase their bottom line?

If you are successful in doing this, then you will have made your product indispensable to your customer / partner and that's the secret to **your long-term success as a product manager**.

Chapter 3

A New Way To Listen To What Your Customers Are Saying About You

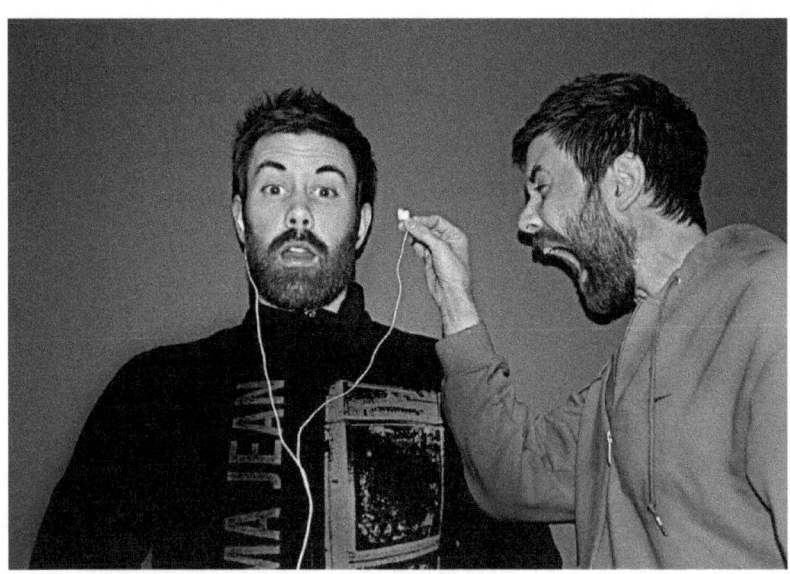

Chapter 3: A New Way To Listen To What Your Customers Are Saying About You

Welcome to the world of the 21st Century – there seems to be a new competitor who is trying to win the attention of your customers every day. What's a product manager to do? The answer lies in getting the message about why your product is better out before your potential customers in a way that **connects with them**. But how? Maybe the answer lies in what your existing customers are saying about your product...

How To Use This New Approach

For years now product managers have been told that we need to **listen to what our customers are telling us** in order to find ways to make our products better. However, nobody has ever really taken the time to tell us what we need to do in order to create product advertising messages that work.

With the arrival of the Internet, **product advertising** is yet one more thing that is undergoing a significant change. For the first time, the Internet gives product managers a chance to "eavesdrop" on what your customers are saying about their experience with your product.

We often think about these types of customer conversations in terms of the negative things that our customers are saying – that's how we can discover what features need to be added to the next version of the product. However, it turns out that **the positive things** that they are saying can help us out also.

New technologies are becoming available that allow the big Internet to be **scanned** in order to collect all of the different things that are being said about your product. This information can reveal just what aspects of your product your customers are talking about ("I like the way that it feels in my hands") as well as what they are not talking about (what? No mention of the extended warrantee that we debated about offering for two months?)

The power of this new approach to creating product ads is allowing your customers to determine what theme you end up using for your next advertising campaign as well as the words and images that you use. Even better, once you've launched the campaign, you can monitor the feedback and **make changes** to it in order to have an even greater impact.

Example: Harrah's Takes A Gamble

A great example of one set of product managers who are doing exactly this comes from the casino company **Harrah's**. Emily Steel has done some research on how they've been using these new tools.

She reports that Harrah's **mined the customer comments** that had been posted on the travel review web site www.TripAdvisor.com along with watching what was being said on Twitter and Facebook in order to determine how they should promote their hotel / casino. What they discovered is that their customers valued the views they could get out of their hotel windows as well has the amenities in their rooms.

Harrah's used this information to change the way that their web site looked as well as changing the types of information that they sent to prospective customers. Since doing this, they've reported that they've seen a **double-digit increase** in the number of on-line bookings for their properties.

What All Of This Means For You

Although this may seem like the way to go in the future, it turns out that you need to **be a bit careful here**. The people who are talking about your product already know about it. You will want to advertise to people who may not already know about your product. This means that things like focus groups and traditional market research are still an important part of what you need to be doing.

Ultimately, as a product manager you need to **add this new technique** for creating advertising that works for your product to your toolbox. It is yet one more way that the Internet is changing everything about the way that product managers do our job...

Chapter 4

How To Tell Your Customer To Stop Using Your Product

Chapter 4: How To Tell Your Customer To Stop Using Your Product

Who among us product managers has not heard about Apple's iPhone product and its incredible retail success? Currently in the U.S. there is only one wireless service provider on who's network these highly desirable phones work: **AT&T's**. You'd think that that was a good thing from an AT&T product manager's point of view, right? Well it turns out that the old saying "too much of a good thing is bad" truly applies in this case...

It turns out that the iPhone, while it's a great phone to use, is a terrible phone to have running on your network. A recent story in the New York Times reported that **AT&T's reputation is taking a severe beating** because of the connectivity problems that iPhone users have been having. What makes this ironic, is that it turns out that the problem isn't really AT&T's but rather how the iPhone was designed!

No matter, AT&T needs to do something and do it quickly. One of the issues that they know that they have to deal with is the problem of customers who love their iPhones just a little bit too much – **the heavy data users**. To deal with this problem, AT&T is planning on taking steps to curtail excessive data usage by these iPhone customers.

From a product manager point-of-view, these users are responsible for much of the growth in wireless data traffic on the AT&T network as well as perceptions of problems with the network. In order to deal with the issue of customers using too much of the available bandwidth to send and receive data from their iPhones, AT&T is thinking about introducing what they are calling **"incentives"** that they hope will encourage customers to cut back on their iPhone data usage.

Just to show how much of a problem the iPhones are causing, a recent study revealed that **the average iPhone user consumes five to seven times more data on a monthly basis** than an average AT&T subscriber who mainly uses their handset for phone calls. Clearly the AT&T product managers have their work cut out for them!

Possible Solutions

What's a product manager to do? The trick here is that AT&T loves to have subscribers. In fact, the more subscribers that they can get to join every month, the better they are doing as a business. The problem is that some of these subscribers **are degrading the quality of service** for the remaining users and people might start unsubscribing because of this.

If we take a look in an AT&T product manager's bag of tricks, the solution that we'll almost immediately stumble across is of course **usage based pricing**. The way that AT&T has their product pricing structured right now, it's almost encouraging iPhone users to send and receive as much data as possible. iPhone users are only required to pay $30 a month for the right to send and receive an unlimited amount of data.

As the AT&T product managers consider their options, they need to be careful that whatever they decide to do they don't end up punishing the majority of their users for the actions of a few data intensive users. They could start to **ration data** like they do for talk minutes and once a user exceeds their monthly allotment amount of data that can be sent or received, then they would start to pay an additional fee.

A more controversial solution is for the AT&T product managers to take things into their own hands and when they detect a heavy data user, they could **start to slow down ("throttle") an iPhone user's connection** if their usage is hurting the network access for nearby users.

What All Of This Means For You

As product managers we are always taught that the more that our customers use our products, the better life will be for us. Clearly, the AT&T product managers have run into **an exception to this rule**. Their next steps have to be taken carefully.

Two levers that they can pull include changing the subscription pricing to encourage the behavior that they want or changing the way that the product works to restrict heavy data user's access. **Both have advantages and disadvantages**.

No matter which option they select, the AT&T product managers need to do something. Nobody ever said that being a product manager was going to be easy and this is a classic example of **why product managers are so valuable...**

Chapter 5

Forget Dating Customers, 5 Ways Product Managers Can Get Real Relationships

Chapter 5: Forget Dating Customers, 5 Ways Product Managers Can Get Real Relationships

How do you measure success for your product? For most product managers this comes down to one number: the number of customers that their product has. However, in today's tough economy, this type of thinking might just be a bit shortsighted. Instead of thinking of all of your product's customers as being a bunch of people that your product is dating, maybe it's time to start to think about what it's going to take **to make your** customers **fall in love with your product**...

The Benefits Of Taking The Long-Term View

Ultimately it's going to be up to your sales team to make the sale. However, as the product manager you are ultimately responsible for getting your product **ready to go on a date with the potential customer**. Just as in real life dating, if you just throw your product out there in front of a prospective customer, who knows what's going to happen (but it's probably not going to be good!)

What should you be doing instead? The first thing that you want to be doing is to set your product up so that **it can get a second date with the potential customer**. How are you going to do this? Simple, you are going to have to work with your sales teams and teach them how to listen to what the customer is saying. Instead of loading them up with product facts, you need to take the time to teach them what to listen for — just what customer problems does your product solve?

In order to make sure that the relationship goes on beyond the first date, you need to make sure that the first contact that a potential customer has with your product (sales call, brochure, web site) doesn't come across like a "sales call" type of conversation. Instead, what you want to do is to **start to build a relationship with them** – show them that your expertise (and your product) can help them solve their problems.

The Right Way To Get A Customer To Partner With Your Product

Dating advice has always been freely available and yet still so many people find that **they struggle to do it correctly**. The same thing can be said about product managers who are looking for ways for their products to get into relationships with new customers.

Although every customer is different, it turns out that there are **five steps** that a product manager can take in order to turn a customer date into a real relationship:

1. **Research and understand a customer's needs:** Just like you wouldn't go on a date without having first done some research on who you are dating, a product manager needs to learn as much as you can about each potential customer. Knowing what their business is and what their needs are will be the key to having a successful date.

2. **Be willing to partner with a customer and become a resource:** anyone can go on a date with a customer – there's no commitment there. If you want it to turn into something more, then you're going to have to make your company a resource that the potential customer can use as a resource.

3. **Become a product success teacher:** nobody ever said that a potential customer is going to know how to date your product either. Although a suitor might think that

they know how to use your product to solve their business problems, they probably don't know all of the ins and outs. This is where a product manager can add value.

4. **Have faith that your product is #1:** at all times you have to be your product's biggest booster. Sure a potential customer may be thinking about dating other products, but you need to keep them focused on developing an exclusive relationship with your product.

5. **Be positive:** you would be amazed at just how important your own attitude is to the success of any relationship that a potential customer might be thinking about developing with your product. If you think highly of your product then it shows and this can make it easier for a suitor to commit.

What All Of This Means For You

Sure customers are nice to have, but getting your product into as many long-term relationships as you can is even better. Having a lot of potential customers date your product is good, but as a product manager you need to find ways to **turn these dates into real relationships / sales.**

To make this happen you will have work with the sales team and teach them to become **good listeners**. What you want to do is to position your company as a resource for a potential customer and your product as a solution to their business needs.

Nobody ever said that this customer / product matchmaking thing was going to be easy. However, if you can do it successfully then you'll have the satisfaction of knowing that you've made the world **just a little bit better** for at least one customer.

Chapter 6

Can Product Managers Know Too Much About Their Customers?

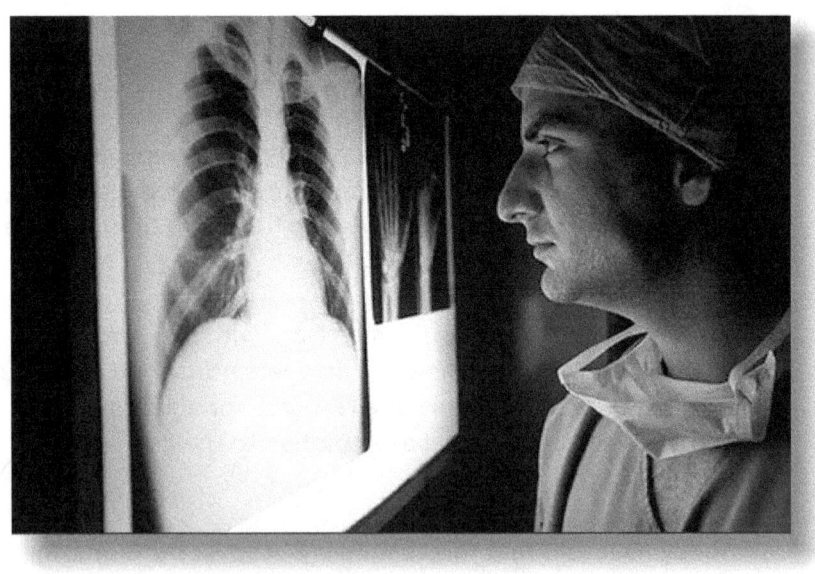

Chapter 6: Can Product Managers Know Too Much About Their Customers?

It's sorta the Holy Grail of product management – to become so **intimate with our customers** that we can almost read their minds. Now while that may sound like a great idea, have any of us taken the time to consider what our customers might be thinking about us doing this?

Information Blending: Good Thing Or Bad Thing?

This whole question about **having lots and lots of information on our customers** has only really started to surface in the past few years as computers have gotten faster and the Internet has made sharing information almost ridiculously easy. However, just because something is easy to do, doesn't necessarily mean that we should be doing it.

Emily Steel reports that a company called EXelate Media is in the process of creating an alliance with a company that we all know: **Nielsen – you know, the company that keeps track of who watches what on TV**. The reason that this announcement is generating so much interest among product managers is because really for the first time, EXelate's captured information on 150 million web surfers will be able to be combined with Nielson's captured behavior information on 115 million American households.

What this means for your customers is that when they go online, now there is the possibility that **they may be seeing very, very targeted ads**. Just think about for a moment: if you know a web surfer's age, race, gender, profession, and marital status and you knew where they had been surfing in the last month or even year, what would your product's ad look like?

The way that EXelate has **collected their information** on your customer's web surfing habits is not really rocket science. What they've done is to strike deals with lots and lots of web sites and then they've scanned all of the registration data that you and I entered when we registered to use those web sites.

They next created **web "cookies"** that are placed on a user's hard drive when they visit one of the sites that they've registered to use. This cookie allows surfers to be identified to other sites that have subscribed to EXelate's service – when you drop by, they can look up a lot of information about you.

The Down Side To Too Much Information

As you may have already guessed, this explosion of personal data being made available to marketers is starting to cause some concerns. The **Federal Trade Commission (FTC)** has started to hold meetings to talk about this very issue.

Just because I like the color purple and I eat lots and lots of lime Jolly Ranchers doesn't mean that I'm going to appreciate seeing ads starting to pop up on my browser for your blue widget product telling me that "4 out of 5" purple loving, line Jolly Rancher eating people have bought your blue widget. In fact, when consumers start to realize that **data is being combined from multiple sources**, they may flat out rebel.

For right now, marketing firms are saying that they understand the issue and that **they handle consumer's personal data very carefully**. They say that no individual can be identified by the data that they have because they've stripped out any identifying info.

What All Of This Means For You

Yes, knowing more about your potential customers is always a good thing for product managers to do. However, in this modern age **it may be possible to know too much about them**.

The arrival of firms that track consumer's online surfing habits and their alliances with traditional consumer behavior tracking firms has created **a super tracker hybrid firm**. All of a sudden, a great deal of information may be known about any customer that visits a web site.

If consumers believe that you know too much about them, **they will push back**. Product manager realize that as with all powerful tools, they are going to have to go slow and make sure that they don't spook their customers by knowing too much...

Chapter 7

What Product Managers Need To Know About Customer Loyalty

Chapter 7: What Product Managers Need To Know About Customer Loyalty

Imagine for a moment that you were in the business of building walls. Every day you'd get up go build part of a wall and then go home. What if every day when you returned, all of the work that you had done the previous day had been undone? How would you ever get that wall built?

Product managers who create products that don't generate customer loyalty find themselves in a situation where every day is like their first day: they have to go out and win every customer for the first time. This is crazy. What you need to do is to find out how to generate loyalty in your customers so that they sell themselves next time it comes to buying your product...

Loyalty Is All About Your Program

The key to a good loyalty program is to have many different layers. Product managers know that customers who have bought from you and are now part of your product's loyalty program will want to move up to the next level if you do this correctly.

In my experience, a product loyalty program needs to have two parts to it: one part that rewards your customers based on how much they've bought from you and another that rewards them for how long they've been your customer.

I like to track how much a customer spends over a 12-month period in order to determine which level of my product's loyalty program they belong in. At the same time, I like to have another loyalty program running that customers can only get included in after they've purchased from me over the past 5 years.

Loyalty Is About Being Remembered

So what should your customers get for being part of your product's loyalty program? Well, that can be very dependent on just exactly what kind of product you are selling. However, there are some basic rules that every product manager needs to follow.

Every member of your product's loyalty program needs to get an annual letter from you, the product manager. You need to thank them for being a customer and let them know what changes are coming up for your product.

During the course of a year, you need to reach out to your loyalty program members at least four times. Depending on what your product is, you need to find ways to provide your loyalty program members with things that they will value. Informational reports, refrigerator magnets, etc.

Don't forget the holidays. I personally believe that sending out Christmas cards is a waste of time and money – everyone else does that. I much prefer (for U.S. based customers) to send out Thanksgiving cards. They are unexpected and will actually be read by your customers.

Loyalty Is Not Slick, It's Personal

Contacting your product's loyalty program members is important, but what is even more important is HOW you contact them. This is the area where I've seen the most product managers fall down.

All too often we can get caught up in how something that our customers are going to see looks. We want it to be a slick and catchy as possible. This is where we start to cause problems.

It has been my experience that communicating with your loyalty program members using plain and relatively simple methods (postal mail, email, web sites) seems to work the best.

What you've got to remember here is that you are working on cultivating a relationship with your repeat buying customers. You're not trying to sell them on your product again, rather you are trying to make them feel like they are a part of your family.

What All Of This Means For You

Product managers who don't set up a customer loyalty program for their products are crazy. You want to make your existing customers feel special and have them take the initiative to maintain the relationship with your product.

There are many ways to set up and run a product loyalty program. Keep in mind that the quality of the program will be determined by the number of membership levels that it has, what you provide your members with, and how you contact them.

Instead of having to keep re-selling your existing customers over and over again, a loyalty program allows you to make them part of your family. Think back to your childhood: isn't it always easier to sell to family members?

Chapter 8

Niche Marketing Requires Product Managers To Personalize Everything

Chapter 8: Niche Marketing Requires Product Managers To Personalize Everything

As product managers we spend a lot of time creating ways to tell customers all about our fantastic product. Too bad that often the brochures, white papers, direct mail, and case studies often fall on deaf ears. It turns out that we're actually doing a couple of things wrong: we're not listening to our customers and we're not talking to them in the way that they want us to. Looks like we've got some work to do here...

Step 1: Find Out How To Talk To Your Customers

When someone buys one of our products, you would think that we'd take the time as part of the purchase process to find out what the best way to contact them in the future would be. However, it turns out that more than often we just get their email and phone number and proceed to use them willy-nilly.

What we should be doing is asking our customers what the best way to contact them is. While we're doing that we should probably also be asking them how often we should be contacting them. I can tell you that too many of us aren't doing either of these things.

The good folks over at Forrester Research did a study in 2009 in which they asked product marketers what contact information they collected on their customers. Here's the depressing information on what they found out:

- 29% captured the type of content that the customer wanted to receive

- 12% captured the customer's desired frequency for receiving emails

- 8% captured the customer's desired frequency for receiving direct mail and telemarketing calls

- 30% of marketers who captured at least one type of preference data took no action based on that customer preference.

Step 2: Personalize Your Communications With Your Customers

I'm going to hope that everyone understands that the more that you personalize your communications with your customers, the better the results of those communications will be. However, all too often product managers either can't or don't pull together the customer information that is needed to do this job well.

The sad part about this is that more often than not we have all the data that we need. However, that data is not stored neatly in one place. Rather it may be spread across multiple databases within the company.

This can include critical personalization information such as when they made their last purchase. If you can't get you hands on this data, then you're going to end up doing the classic ineffective marketing technique of sending out product information in a "spray and pray" fashion.

Example: The Ford F-150 Pickup Truck

An example of how to do things correctly comes from the Ford motor company's product managers. They wanted to offer their extended warrantee product to their F-150 pickup truck customers; however, their impersonal approach in which they simply used the customer's name just wasn't doing the trick: they had a 2.5% response rate.

Determined to make their customer contact more personal, the Ford product managers went back to the company's databases and pulled together all of the information that they could on the people who had bought their F-150 truck. This included things such as vehicle type, how long they had owned it, address, age, income and gender.

Using this type of information they were able to personalize how they interacted with each customer. This went so far as being able to send them material that contained a picture of a correct gender person standing in front of the correct model F-150 which was painted the same color as the customer's.

By doing this, Ford saw a 5.7% increase in their response rates and a whopping 35.7% increase in their sales penetration. Not bad results for what was basically some behind-the-scenes database work.

What All Of This Means For You

Product managers will forever be responsible for creating material that will be used to interact with your customers. As long as you are going to go to the effort of creating these flyers, white papers, mailers, etc., you may as well make them as effective as possible.

The best way to do this is to take steps to personalize your interaction with your customers. You can start doing this by collecting information on how they want you to contact them. Additionally you'll want to find out how often they are willing to allow you to reach out to them. Finally, you'll need to pull together all of the information that your company has on your customers and use that when creating material to send to them.

Personalizing your interaction with your customers is not impossible to do. However, it does take some work on your part and you will need to collect data that may be stored in multiple locations. Take the time to do this right and the rewards will make the effort well worth your time.

Chapter 9

Why Product Managers Need To Learn To Love Their Crazy Customers

Chapter 9: Why Product Managers Need To Learn To Love Their Crazy Customers

Just who are you hoping that will buy your product? Sane, rational people who you'd be more than willing to invite over to your place for dinner? Or perhaps stark raving mad folks whom you'd probably cross to the other side of the street were you to encounter them in public? I'm guessing that you'd probably pick the sane folks, but maybe you'd be wrong...

What Makes A Customer A "Crazy Customer"?

With a little luck, your product already has a lot of customers. Not all of these customers can be considered to be "crazy customers". But some of them most defiantly are.

Just what makes a customer a crazy customer can vary from product to product, but the consumer researcher Dr. Andreas Eisingerich has identified the following characteristics that they all seem to share:

- They personally identify with your product and gain some meaning in their life from it.

- They are willing to defend your product against attacks that show up in the media or from competitors.

- They describe your product as being "part of the family".

- They display extreme behavior in relation to your product (think about waiting in line for days when new models to become available).

- They believe that "... buying cheap is expensive" and will continue to buy your product even if it is not the most inexpensive.

Why Crazy Customers Are The Ones That You Want To Have

Dr. Eisingerich's research shows that only about 5% of your customers will turn out to be crazy customers. However, this small group of customer is good to have on your side.

First off, they are very loyal to your product. No matter what changes that you make to your product they will be the ones who stick with it. They are also willing to speak up and defend your product when others attack it.

These are also the customers who have the resources needed to buy your product. More often than not they turn out to be between 30 and 45 years old and make more money than the national average for where they live.

Finally, they are willing to add value to your product. They will convince others to use your product and they will often come up with novel ways to incorporate your product in other parts of their life.

What Do Product Managers Need To Do For Crazy Customers

Sadly, studies show that 82% of product managers have not spent any time thinking about how they can leverage their crazy customers to make their products more successful. In fact, only 8% of product managers are currently targeting these customers. Looks like it's time for you to get on board.

Let Crazy Customers Own Your Product: Taking the time to set up opportunities for your customers to create communities around your product is a great way to allow your crazy customers to come together and interact. Allowing them to make suggestions and even customize the look & feel of your product can get them to feel as though they are involved in the product creation process

Ask For Input From Your Crazy Customers: Product managers are always looking for suggestions on where to take their products next. Since crazy customers use your product so extensively, they can be a great source of input on what new features you should be considering.

Capture Crazy Customer's Stories: What can convince more people to buy your product will be the stories of how others use it and what problems it has solved for them. Asking your crazy customers to share their stories with you can provide a rich set of material for communicating with future potential customers.

What All Of This Means For You

Product managers want as many customers for their product as possible. Along with regular customers come the crazy customers. Product managers have to make a decision here: to ignore the crazy ones or to adjust their marketing efforts to address this group.

Finding ways to meet the needs of your crazy customers can yield great benefits for your product. They can attract new customers and they can provide you with great inputs for new features and marketing stories.

The one thing that you don't want to do is to ignore your crazy customers. You've worked hard enough to create a product that has attracted them, now make sure that you find ways to get your crazy customers to share their devotion to your product with others...

Chapter 10

What A High-End NYC Salon Can Teach Product Managers

Chapter 10: What A High-End NYC Salon Can Teach Product Managers

Just imagine the perfect world for a product manager: you have you choice of high end customers, they really don't care just how expensive your product is – they feel that **they must have it at any price**, and your sales are virtually global recession-proof. Sound impossible? Well it's not for one high-end New York City salon and although you might not be in the business of making women look beautiful, I'm willing to bet that you could learn a thing or two from this place...

Welcome To The Pierre Michel Salon

Right off the bat, let's all admit something here: going to a salon is never a required part of anyone's day. However, there sure seem to be a lot of people who truly feel as though **they couldn't live without this little indulgence**.

The Pierre Michel Salon in New York City is one such salon. It is in such high demand that **it is easily able to fill a large location** in one of the most expensive cities in the world all the while becoming more and more successful.

Wendy Lee from the New York Times recently spent some time looking into what makes the Pierre Michel salon so successful. What she found is **valuable information for every product manager**.

This salon employs 75 beauticians. This is important because each of these beauticians has their own client base who adores them and **keeps coming back time after time**. While in the salon, the clients visit one of the 61 workstations (no, not like the kind of workstations that you are thinking about) where they can have work done on their hair, face, and hands.

The relationship between the salon and its customers is so close that when customers show up, **they almost never bother to sign in**. Instead, they head back to the workstation where they'll be worked on without stopping. The salon classifies its customers according to if they are new, regulars, or VERY regulars.

In order for any salon to stay in business, they need to have **a steady stream of customers**. At the Pierre Michel salon on a summer day they service an average of about 245 clients. During their busy season, they can service up to 400 clients per day!

What Makes This Salon So Special?

So what makes this Pierre Michel salon any different from that SuperCuts down the corner from where you live? **It starts with the folks who own and run the place**: Pierre Ouaknine and Michel Obadia. They immigrated from Morocco back in the 1970's and have been hard at work making people look good ever since.

In Pierre's office he has a bank of **close circuit television screens** that allow him to keep close tabs on each of the workstations in the salon. He spends his time watching them in order to make sure that his staff is not just doing their jobs, but rather taking the time to actually pamper their clients.

We all know that in order for a product to be successful **you need to make money selling it**. This is yet another area where the Pierre Michel salon does a fantastic job. A basic women's haircut will run you $175 (a man's haircut costs $115 but includes nose, ears, and brows trimming). Hair coloring costs about $300. You get the point. Oh, and don't forget the 20% tip for your beautician and of course some sort of tip for everyone who assisted them.

Why do so many New Yorkers come to this salon? According to Sue Ellen Gifford (an eyebrow guru) they realize that it takes **three things** to look good in New York: eyes, teeth, and hair.

Pierre Michel succeeds because they've **expanded their client base** to also include men. They get haircuts, etc. at the salon because just like the ladies they want to look their best.

The salon realizes that **the most precious resource** that their customers have is time. That's why they've installed wireless Internet access. Amazingly enough this allows their clients to keep working even while they are being treated.

Finally, the success of the Pierre Michel salon comes down to one thing: **relationships**. Unlike at that SuperCuts that you may go to, at this salon you'll see your favorite stylist over and over again. In fact, many customers have been seeing the same stylist for decades – how's that for customer loyalty?

What All Of This Means For You

Every product manager can learn from the Pierre Michel Salon's success. Clearly they are a runaway success and there are several things that they can **teach every product manager**.

We all like to pay lip service to **the idea of customer service**, but the Pierre Michel salon lives and dies by how good of a job they do on this. Oh, and they do a really good job. Instead of creating a service that they require their customers to conform to, instead they've made the services that they offer bend and fit their customer's busy lives.

By doing this they've created a product that not only sells well in good times, but **also sells well during global recessions**. Product managers who spend too much time focusing on how a web site looks or producing even more product brochures and not enough time on customer service, need to pay attention. Spending time to make your customer feel beautiful about using your product can pay handsome rewards...

Chapter 11

Product Managers Realize That They Are Really Selling To Grandparents

Chapter 11: Product Managers Realize That They Are Really Selling To Grandparents

Who is the customer for your product? Maybe a better question is **how old is your target customer?** It turns out that they may be much older than any of us have realized – America's grandparents are becoming the dominate consumer force (and this relates to business to business transactions also). Is your product ready?

Just The Facts Please – The Arrival Of The Grandparents

So how did the people that we're selling our products to get so old all of a sudden? Well, it turns out that **this has been going on for quite some time**. Ever since 2000 the spending levels by grandparents has grown by a whopping 7.6% per year. This is almost double the annual overall consumer growth rate!

The web site Grandparents.com recently did a study of this group of U.S. consumers. They discovered that the group **contains more than 70M members** and that unlike the grandparents that came before them, they are both better educated and spend more.

This is a large group. The grandparent group is larger than either the Hispanic or African-American populations in the U.S.

How much do they spend you may be asking. Well, according to the study **they are currently spending more that US$100B on entertainment alone**. This includes everything from vehicles (boats and bikes) to gear (cameras and tents).

It's not just entertainment that this group is spending on. They are also doing a lot of traveling. This is evidenced by the simple fact that **they spend US$77B on all things travel related**: tickets, hotels, food, etc.

Taken all together, **the grandparent group is a huge purchasing group**. They spend a total of US$2 Trillion every year on goods and services. Just to put this into perspective, that is 1/3 of overall U.S. consumer spending by just one group of consumers.

Ultimately how much the grandparents have to spend is determined by **how much money they have**. It appears as though they have a great deal. In houses that were led by 55-64 year olds their average net worth was US$254,000. This is the highest value of any current age group.

What You Need To Do With Your Product To Sell To Grandparents

Not all products that we manage will be sold to grandparents. However, we need to understand that **grandparents are probably somewhere there in the equation**. Even if the initial purchasers of our products are not grandparents themselves, then there's a good chance that they are serving grandparents using our products.

There are a number of different things that we can do that will **make it easier to sell our products to this enormous group of consumers**. One of the most important things to understand is that these customers don't feel as old as they are. This means that you need to make sure that you don't use words or images that convey the idea that they are old or infirm.

On top of doing this, you should make sure that your marketing efforts are doing the things that you should already be doing. This means that you need to make sure that **the message that your product is conveying is honest**. You want your potential customers to view your product as being authentic.

As always, you are going to want to **show your customers the benefits of your product**. The trick here however is that you are going to want to do this in a way that is ageless. If you can make sure that you are sending your marketing messages to the right people, then you'll be able to successfully tap into the largest group of potential customers for your product that's out there!

What All Of This Means To You

The people that we sell our products to **have been gradually becoming older**. Now as a generation the people controlling the purse strings of 1/3 of consumer spending overall are a part of the grandparent generation.

Product managers need to realize that our customer base may have become older on us. We're going to have to **adjust how we market our products** to appeal to this segment – and make sure to not upset them!

Much of what we should be doing as Product Managers should help us appeal to this customer demographic. If we are **honest with our customers**, focus our marketing efforts on our product's benefits and stay away from calling our customers old then our products will be successful.

Chapter 12

Product Managers Don't Like Surprises: Know Your Product's Customers!

Chapter 12: Product Managers Don't Like Surprises: Know Your Product's Customers!

I find myself telling the product managers that I'm working with that they need to understand that one of a product manager's most important jobs is to **give good direction to their sales teams**: who will buy your product. You may think that you know the answer, but like the product managers for 5-Hour Energy Shots you might be wrong...

The 5-Hour Energy Shot Customer Surprise

Have you heard about the energy shot products? These are drinks that come with names that would make any product manager who has ever done branding **become instantly envious**: "6 Hour Power", "Nitro2Go", "ZipFizz" and of course, the market leader "5 Hour Energy".

These products are **loaded with caffeine stimulants** and a bunch of other stuff (vitamins and herbs). The promise is that they will allow the drinker to stay alert for hours after drinking one.

As a product manager, who do you think that **the audience** for this type of product would be? Just on a gut level, you'd think that probably students and people who work long hours (think truckers and police) would make up your target customers. You'd be right, sort of.

For you see, it turns out that the brand managers at all of these energy booster shot products seem to have **overlooked** a very large and important market: senior citizens.

How You Can Make Sure That You Are Not Surprised

What's happened is that they have just recently come to realize that all of those **Baby Boomers** who are starting to get close to retirement age don't want to slow down.

The brand mangers didn't really do any big market study to find this out. Rather **stories started to get back to them**. It was little things, like big spikes in sales when the product just happened to be located right next to a product that senior citizens were buying (like wrinkle cream) in a store like Costco it would sell out.

Once they started to realize that there might be something here, they started to use **a proven communication channel**, the American Association of Retired People (AARP) to reach this demographic. They ran ads in their magazines and attended their trade shows and handed out products.

Clearly, the energy shot brand managers had **a huge potential market** sitting right under their noses for a long time before they realized that it was there. How can you prevent this from happening to your product?

The key is to keep your eyes open and take a look at the **sales of your product** – the sales people will only care about making the sale, you need to care about how much was sold and who bought it.

It turns out that **if there is a dip in sales of your product**, that can tell you a lot also. You have some assumptions about how much of your product will be sold and to whom it will be sold. If that's not happening, then you need to take a closer look and find out where your thinking went wrong.

What All Of This Means For You

As product and brand managers, we are responsible for identifying **who we are going to sell our products to**. The energy shot product mangers thought that they had done a good job of doing this, however, their market came back and told them that they had overlooked a very large segment.

In the case of the energy shot product, the senior citizen market **had a huge need for their product** – they don't want to slow down and they view the product as being able to help them keep going. Once the product managers realized that this market existed, they were able to adjust their marketing and start to address it.

As product managers we need to make sure that we are not **overlooking large segments of untapped customers** for our products. Carefully looking at who is buying our products and making sure that we investigate unexpected peaks and dips can reveal untapped customer segments. That should give you something to think about the next time you are chugging one of those energy shots!

It's from the forge of failure that the steel of success is formed.

Hard Work Does Not Guarantee Success, But Success Does Not Happen Without Hard Work.

- Dr. Jim Anderson

Create Products Your Customers Want At A Price That They Are Willing To Pay!

Dr. Jim Anderson is available to provide training and coaching on the two topics that are the most important to product managers everywhere: how do I create the products that my customers want and what should I price them at?

Dr. Anderson believes that in order to both learn and remember what he says, product managers need to laugh. Each one of his speeches is full of fun and humor so that what he says "sticks" with everyone.

Dr. Anderson's Product Management Training Includes:

1. How can you segment your market?
2. What problems are your customers having right now?
3. Which of your customer's problems does your product solve?
4. How much of this problem does your product solve?
5. How much will it cost your customer if they don't fix this problem?

Dr. Jim Anderson presents over 100 speeches per year. To invite Dr. Anderson to speak at your event, contact him at:

Phone: 813-418-6970 or
Email: jim@BlueElephantConsulting.com

Blue
Elephant
Consulting

Speaking.   Negotiating.   Managing.   Marketing.

Photo Credits:

Cover - By: Epic Fireworks.
https://www.flickr.com/photos/epicfireworks/

Chapter 1 - By: Bill Alldredge
https://www.flickr.com/photos/billypalooza/

Chapter 2 – By: Tom Simpson
https://www.flickr.com/photos/randar/

Chapter 3 – By: Jonathan Powell
https://www.flickr.com/photos/metrojp/

Chapter 4 – By: Mike Mozart
https://www.flickr.com/photos/jeepersmedia/

Chapter 5 - Tristan Schmurr
https://www.flickr.com/photos/kewl/

Chapter 6 – By: galleryquantum
https://www.flickr.com/photos/32490173@N05/

Chapter 7 – By: Matt Deavenport
https://www.flickr.com/photos/paradisecoastie/

Chapter 8 – By: Chris Blakeley
https://www.flickr.com/photos/csb13/

Chapter 9 –By: StarMama
https://www.flickr.com/photos/thestarmama/

Chapter 10 – By: Luc
https://www.flickr.com/photos/pittou2/

Chapter 11 – By: Ben Smith
https://www.flickr.com/photos/dotbenjamin/

Chapter 12 – By: Mike Mozart
https://www.flickr.com/photos/jeepersmedia/

Other Books By The Author

Product Management

- Product Management Secrets: Techniques For Product Managers To Boost Product Sales And Increase Customer Satisfaction

- Product Development Lessons For Product Managers: How Product Managers Can Create Successful Products

- Customer Lessons For Product Managers: Techniques For Product Managers To Better Understand What Their Customers Really Want

- Product Failure Lessons For Product Managers: Examples Of Products That Have Failed For Product Managers To Learn From

- Communication Skills For Product Managers: The Communication Skills That Product Managers Need To Know How To Use In Order To Have A Successful Product

- How To Have A Successful Product Manager Career: The Things That You Need To Be Doing

TODAY In Order To Have A Successful Product Manager Career

- Product Manager Product Success: How to keep your product on track and make it become a success

Public Speaking

- Secrets To Organizing A Speech For Maximum Impact: How to put together a speech that will capture and hold your audience's attention

- How To Become A Better Speaker By Changing How You Speak: Change techniques that will transform a speech into a memorable event

- How To Give A Great Presentation: Presentation techniques that will transform a speech into a memorable event

- How To Rehearse In Order To Give The Perfect Speech: How to effectively rehearse your next speech to that your message be remembered forever!

- Secrets To Creating The Perfect Speech: How to create a speech that will make your message be remembered forever!

- Secrets To Organizing The Perfect Speech: How to organize the best speech of your life!

- Secrets To Planning The Perfect Speech: How to plan to give the best speech of your life

- How To Show What You Mean During A Presentation: How to use visual techniques to transform a speech into a memorable event

CIO Skills

- What CIOs Need To Know About Working With Partners: Techniques For CIOs To Use In Order To Be Able To Successfully Work With Partners

- Critical CIO Management Skills: Decision Making Skills That Every CIO Needs To Have In Order To Be Able To Make The Right Choices

- How CIOs Can Make Innovation Happen: Tips And Techniques For CIOs To Use In Order To Make Innovation Happen In Their IT Department

- CIO Communication Skills Secrets: Tips And Techniques For CIOs To Use In Order To Become

Better Communicators

- Managing Your CIO Career: Steps That CIOs Have To Take In Order To Have A Long And Successful Career

- CIO Business Skills: How CIOs can work effectively with the rest of the company!

IT Manager Skills

- Growing Your CIO Career: How CIOs Can Work With The Entire Company In Order To Be Successful

- How IT Managers Can Make Innovation Happen: Tips And Techniques For IT Managers To Use In Order To Make Innovation Happen In Their Teams

- Staffing Skills IT Managers Must Have: Tips And Techniques That IT Managers Can Use In Order To Correctly Staff Their Teams

- Secrets Of Effective Leadership For IT Managers: Tips And Techniques That IT Managers Can Use In Order To Develop Leadership Skills

- IT Manager Career Secrets: Tips And Techniques That IT Managers Can Use In Order To Have A Successful Career

- IT Manager Budgeting Skills: How IT Managers Can Request, Manage, Use, And Track Their Funding

- Secrets Of Managing Budgets: What IT Managers Need To Know In Order To Understand How Their Company Uses Money

Negotiating

- Learn How To Signal In Your Next Negotiation: How To Develop The Skill Of Effective Signaling In A Negotiation In Order To Get The Best Possible Outcome

- Learn The Skill Of Exploring In A Negotiation: How To Develop The Skill Of Exploring What Is Possible In A Negotiation In Order To Reach The Best Possible Deal

- Learn How To Argue In Your Next Negotiation: How To Develop The Skill Of Effective Arguing In A Negotiation In Order To Get The Best Possible Outcome

- How To Open Your Next Negotiation: How To Start A Negotiation In Order To Get The Best Possible Outcome

- Preparing For Your Next Negotiation: What You Need To Do BEFORE A Negotiation Starts In Order To Get The Best Possible Deal

- Learn How To Package Trades In Your Next Negotiation

- All Good Things Come To An End: How To Close A Negotiation - How To Develop The Skill Of Closing In Order To Get The Best Possible Outcome From A Negotiation

Miscellaneous

- The Internet-Enabled Successful School District Superintendent: How To Use The Internet To Boost Parental Involvement In Your Schools

- Power Distribution Unit (PDU) Secrets: What Everyone Who Works In A Data Center Needs To Know!

- Making The Jump: How To Land Your Dream Job When You Get Out Of College!

- How To Use The Internet To Create Successful Students And Involved Parents

Techniques For Product Managers To Better Understand What Their Customers Really Want

This book has been written with one goal in mind – to show you how to find out what your customers really want from your product. We're going to show you how to listen to what your customers are really telling you.

Let's Make Your Product A Success!

What You'll Find Inside:

- **HOW TO MOVE FROM CUSTOMERS TO PARTNERS**

- **WHAT PRODUCT MANAGERS NEED TO KNOW ABOUT CUSTOMER LOYALTY**

- **WHY PRODUCT MANAGERS NEED TO LEARN TO LOVE THEIR CRAZY CUSTOMERS**

- **PRODUCT MANAGERS DON'T LIKE SURPRISES: KNOW YOUR PRODUCT'S CUSTOMERS!**

Dr. Jim Anderson brings his 4 college degrees coupled with over 25 years of real-world experience to this book. He's managed products at some of the world's largest firms as well as at start-ups. He's going to show you what you need to do in order to make your career a success!

www.ingramcontent.com/pod-product-compliance
Lightning Source LLC
Chambersburg PA
CBHW070848180526
45168CB00002B/998